Google Docs Essentials

Your Complete Guide to Document
Creation and Collaboration

Laine Griffey

Laine Griffey
521 Concord Avenue
Elkhart, Indiana 46516

Introduction to Google Docs

Purpose of Google Docs

Google Docs is a powerful, cloud-based word processing application that enables users to create, edit, and collaborate on documents in real time. It offers a wide range of functionalities, from basic text formatting to advanced document automation, making it a versatile tool for both personal and professional use. Whether you're drafting a report, creating a collaborative project, or preparing a mail merge for a book promotion, Google Docs provides the tools you need to organize and present your content effectively.

Key Features of Google Docs

1. **Cloud-Based Accessibility:**
   - Access your documents from anywhere with an internet connection. All changes are saved automatically in real-time, ensuring that your work is always up-to-date.
2. **Collaboration:**
   - Multiple users can work on the same document simultaneously. You can see changes made by others in real-time, leave comments, and chat within the document, enhancing teamwork and productivity.
3. **Integration with Google Workspace:**
   - Google Docs seamlessly integrates with other Google Workspace apps like Google Sheets, Google Slides, Google Forms, and Google Drive. This integration allows for

easy data sharing and workflow automation across different tools.

4. **Templates:**
   - Google Docs offers a variety of templates for common tasks such as resumes, letters, reports, and more. These templates can help you get started quickly and ensure that your documents are well-organized and professional-looking.

5. **Mobile Compatibility:**
   - The Google Docs mobile app allows you to view and edit your documents on the go, providing flexibility and convenience for mobile users.

6. **Data Security:**
   - Google Docs includes robust security features such as two-factor authentication, encryption, and granular sharing permissions to protect your data.

Overview of Document Creation and Collaboration Capabilities

Google Docs comes equipped with numerous features that facilitate document creation and collaboration. Users can format text using a wide array of tools, insert images and tables, and automate repetitive tasks with macros. The ability to collaborate with others in real-time also makes it an excellent choice for team projects. Additionally, its integration with other Google Workspace apps and various add-ons extends its functionality beyond a traditional word processor.

Key Document Creation and Collaboration Features

1. **Text Formatting and Styles:**
   - Google Docs supports a wide range of text formatting options, including font styles, sizes, colors, and paragraph alignment. You can also create and apply custom styles to ensure consistency throughout your document.
2. **Insert Images, Tables, and Links:**
   - Enhance your documents by inserting images, tables, and links. Google Docs allows you to easily add and format these elements to create visually appealing and informative content.
3. **Comments and Suggestions:**
   - Collaborators can leave comments and suggestions directly within the document. This feature is essential for peer reviews, editing, and collaborative projects, ensuring that feedback is clear and actionable.
4. **Revision History:**
   - Google Docs automatically saves versions of your document. You can view the revision history to see changes made over time, who made them, and revert to previous versions if needed.
5. **Voice Typing:**
   - Use the voice typing feature to dictate text directly into your document. This can be a time-saver for users who prefer speaking over typing.
6. **Add-ons and Integrations:**
   - Extend the functionality of Google Docs with add-ons and integrations. Popular add-ons include Grammarly for grammar checking,

DocuSign for electronic signatures, and Google Translate for translating text. Integrations with tools like Zapier and IFTTT can automate workflows and connect Google Docs with other apps.

7. **Scripting and Automation:**
   - Google Apps Script enables you to write custom scripts to automate tasks and enhance the functionality of your documents. You can create custom functions, automate repetitive tasks, and integrate with other Google Workspace apps.

Practical Applications

1. **Report Writing:**
   - Draft detailed reports with embedded charts, tables, and images. Use collaborative features to gather input from multiple team members and streamline the review process.
2. **Project Documentation:**
   - Create comprehensive project documentation with section headings, lists, and tables. Collaborate in real-time to keep all stakeholders informed and up-to-date.
3. **Marketing Materials:**
   - Design brochures, flyers, and other marketing materials using Google Docs' rich formatting options and templates. Collaborate with your marketing team to ensure consistency and quality.
4. **Meeting Minutes:**

- Record meeting minutes efficiently with predefined templates and real-time collaboration. Share the document with attendees immediately after the meeting for quick reference.

5. **Educational Tools:**
   - Teachers can use Google Docs to create lesson plans, assignments, and quizzes. Collaborative features allow students to work on group projects and receive feedback from their peers and instructors.

6. **Mail Merge for Marketing:**
   - Automate personalized email campaigns by merging data from Google Sheets with email templates in Gmail. Track engagement metrics and analyze campaign performance.

Google Docs is a versatile and powerful tool for document creation and collaboration. Its cloud-based nature, real-time collaboration capabilities, and extensive range of features make it an excellent choice for both personal and professional use. Whether you're drafting a simple letter or creating complex project documentation, Google Docs provides the functionality and flexibility you need to get the job done efficiently and effectively.

Text Formatting and Styles

Proper text formatting and style management are crucial for creating professional and easily readable documents. Google Docs offers a wide array of formatting tools to help you customize the appearance of your text and maintain consistency throughout your document.

Basic Formatting

1. **Font Styles and Sizes:**
   - **Changing Font Style:**
     - Highlight the text you want to change.
     - Click the font dropdown in the toolbar and select the desired font.
   - **Adjusting Font Size:**
     - Highlight the text you want to resize.
     - Click the font size dropdown in the toolbar and select the desired size.
2. **Text Color and Highlighting:**
   - **Changing Text Color:**
     - Highlight the text you want to change.
     - Click the text color button in the toolbar and choose the desired color.
   - **Highlighting Text:**
     - Highlight the text you want to highlight.
     - Click the highlight color button in the toolbar and choose the desired highlight color.
3. **Paragraph Alignment and Spacing:**

- Aligning Text:
    - Select the paragraph you want to align.
    - Click the alignment buttons in the toolbar (left, center, right, justify) to align the text accordingly.
- Adjusting Line Spacing:
    - Select the paragraph you want to adjust.
    - Click the line spacing button in the toolbar and choose the desired spacing option (single, 1.15, 1.5, double).

Advanced Formatting

1. **Creating and Applying Custom Styles:**
    - Creating a Custom Style:
        - Format a piece of text with the desired attributes (font, size, color, etc.).
        - Highlight the formatted text, click the styles dropdown in the toolbar, and select "Normal text."
        - Click "Update 'Normal text' to match."
    - Applying a Custom Style:
        - Highlight the text you want to format.
        - Click the styles dropdown in the toolbar and select the custom style you created.
2. **Using Headers and Footers:**
    - Inserting a Header or Footer:
        - Click "Insert" in the menu bar.

- Select "Headers & footers" and choose either "Header" or "Footer."
  - **Customizing Headers and Footers:**
    - Click inside the header or footer area to add text or elements.
    - Use the formatting tools to customize the appearance of the header or footer.
3. **Adding Page Numbers:**
   - **Inserting Page Numbers:**
     - Click "Insert" in the menu bar.
     - Select "Page numbers" and choose the desired positioning and format.
   - **Customizing Page Numbers:**
     - Click on the inserted page number to format it using the toolbar options.

By mastering these basic and advanced formatting techniques, you can ensure that your documents are visually appealing, consistent, and professional. In the next section, we'll explore how to insert and work with various elements in Google Docs, such as images, tables, and links.

Inserting Elements

Enhancing your documents with images, tables, and links can make them more informative and visually appealing. Google Docs provides easy-to-use tools for inserting and formatting these elements.

Adding Images and Drawings

1. **Inserting Images:**
   - **From Your Computer:**
     - Click "Insert" in the menu bar.
     - Select "Image" and then "Upload from computer."
     - Choose the image file from your computer and click "Open."
   - **From the Web:**
     - Click "Insert" in the menu bar.
     - Select "Image" and then "Search the web."
     - Use the search bar to find an image and click "Insert."
2. **Using the Drawing Tool:**
   - **Creating a Drawing:**
     - Click "Insert" in the menu bar.
     - Select "Drawing" and then "New."
     - Use the drawing tools (e.g., shapes, text boxes) to create your drawing.
     - Click "Save and Close" to insert the drawing into your document.
   - **Editing a Drawing:**
     - Click on the drawing in your document.

- Click "Edit" to open the Drawing tool and make changes.
- Click "Save and Close" to update the drawing in your document.

Working with Tables

1. **Inserting and Formatting Tables:**
   - **Inserting a Table:**
     - Click "Insert" in the menu bar.
     - Select "Table" and choose the desired number of rows and columns.
   - **Formatting a Table:**
     - Click on the table to select it.
     - Use the table toolbar to adjust the border color, background color, and other formatting options.
2. **Merging and Splitting Cells:**
   - **Merging Cells:**
     - Highlight the cells you want to merge.
     - Right-click and select "Merge cells."
   - **Splitting Cells:**
     - Click on the merged cell.
     - Right-click and select "Unmerge cells."

Inserting Links and Bookmarks

1. **Adding Hyperlinks:**
   - **Inserting a Link:**
     - Highlight the text you want to turn into a link.

- Click the link button in the toolbar (or press Ctrl+K).
- Enter the URL in the dialog box and click "Apply."
  - **Editing or Removing a Link:**
    - Click on the linked text.
    - Click the link button in the toolbar to edit the URL or click "Remove" to delete the link.

2. **Creating Bookmarks for Easy Navigation:**
   - **Inserting a Bookmark:**
     - Place your cursor where you want to add the bookmark.
     - Click "Insert" in the menu bar and select "Bookmark."
   - **Linking to a Bookmark:**
     - Highlight the text you want to link.
     - Click the link button in the toolbar.
     - Select "Bookmarks" and choose the bookmark you want to link to.

By using these tools to insert and manage images, tables, and links, you can create more engaging and organized documents. In the next section, we'll cover how to use comments and suggestions to collaborate effectively with others in Google Docs.

Comments and Suggestions

Collaborating on documents is one of the key strengths of Google Docs. Comments and suggestions enable multiple users to provide feedback, make edits, and communicate effectively within the document.

Adding and Managing Comments

1. **Inserting Comments:**
   - **Highlighting Text:**
     - Select the text or place the cursor where you want to add a comment.
     - Click the comment button in the toolbar (or press Ctrl+Alt+M).
     - Type your comment in the dialog box and click "Comment."
   - **Replying to Comments:**
     - Click on the comment to expand it.
     - Type your reply in the reply box and press Enter.
2. **Resolving and Deleting Comments:**
   - **Resolving Comments:**
     - Once a comment has been addressed, click "Resolve" to mark it as resolved. Resolved comments are hidden but can be viewed by clicking "Comments" in the top-right corner and selecting "See all comments."
   - **Deleting Comments:**
     - Click on the comment to expand it.

- Click the three dots in the top-right corner of the comment box and select "Delete."

Using Suggestion Mode

1. **Making Suggested Edits:**
   - **Activating Suggestion Mode:**
     - Click the editing mode dropdown in the top-right corner (next to the "Share" button) and select "Suggesting."
   - **Suggesting Changes:**
     - Make edits to the document as you normally would. Your changes will appear as suggestions, highlighted in green, with the original text remaining visible.
   - **Commenting on Suggestions:**
     - You can add comments to your suggestions by highlighting the suggested text and clicking the comment button.
2. **Accepting or Rejecting Suggestions:**
   - **Reviewing Suggestions:**
     - Click on any suggestion to see the proposed changes.
   - **Accepting Suggestions:**
     - Click the checkmark button next to the suggestion to accept it and apply the changes to the document.
   - **Rejecting Suggestions:**
     - Click the X button next to the suggestion to reject it and discard the proposed changes.

By using comments and suggestions, you can facilitate effective collaboration, ensure clear communication, and streamline the editing process. In the next section, we'll explore the revision history feature to track changes and restore previous versions of your document.

Revision History

Google Docs automatically saves versions of your document, allowing you to track changes, see who made them, and revert to previous versions if needed. This feature is crucial for maintaining a record of edits and ensuring that you can recover previous work if necessary.

Viewing and Restoring Versions

1. **Accessing Version History:**
   - **Opening Version History:**
     - Click "File" in the menu bar.
     - Select "Version history," then "See version history" (or press Ctrl+Alt+Shift+H).
   - **Navigating Version History:**
     - A panel will appear on the right side of the screen, displaying a list of document versions. Each version is timestamped and labeled with the editor's name.
2. **Viewing Changes:**
   - **Exploring Versions:**
     - Click on any version in the panel to view the document as it was at that point in time. Changes made in each version are highlighted, with different colors representing different editors.
   - **Detailed View:**
     - Expand the version history by clicking the arrow next to a version date to see more detailed changes within that timeframe.

3. **Naming and Restoring Versions:**
   - **Naming Versions:**
     - Click the three dots next to a version date in the version history panel.
     - Select "Name this version" and enter a descriptive name to make it easier to identify specific versions later.
   - **Restoring Versions:**
     - To revert to a previous version, click on the desired version in the panel.
     - Click "Restore this version" at the top of the document. The document will revert to the selected version, and the current version will be saved in the version history.

By utilizing the revision history feature, you can effectively manage and track changes to your document, ensuring that all edits are recorded and recoverable. In the next section, we'll discuss how to set up and manage notifications to stay informed about document changes and comments.

Using Notifications

Google Docs allows you to set up notifications to stay informed about changes and comments in your documents. This feature is particularly useful for keeping track of collaborative projects and ensuring you don't miss important updates.

Set Up and Manage Notifications

1. **Enabling Email Notifications:**
   - **Access Notification Settings:**
     - Click on the "Comments" button in the top-right corner of the document.
     - Select "Notification settings."
   - **Choose Notification Preferences:**
     - In the dialog box, choose your preferred notification settings:
       - **All comments and replies:** Receive an email for every comment and reply.
       - **Comments that mention you:** Receive an email only when you are mentioned.
       - **None:** Turn off email notifications.
     - Click "OK" to save your settings.
2. **Managing Notification Rules:**
   - **Create Notification Rules:**
     - Click "Tools" in the menu bar.
     - Select "Notification rules."
   - **Set Notification Criteria:**
     - In the dialog box, choose the criteria for notifications:

- **When changes are made:** Receive notifications for any changes in the document.
- **When collaborators are added or removed:** Receive notifications when users are added or removed.
- Choose the frequency of notifications:
  - **Email - right away:** Receive immediate notifications.
  - **Email - daily digest:** Receive a summary of notifications once a day.
- Click "Save" to create the notification rule.

By setting up and managing notifications, you can stay updated on document changes and comments, ensuring that you remain engaged and informed in collaborative projects. In the next section, we'll explore the voice typing feature to help you dictate text directly into your document.

Voice Typing

Voice typing in Google Docs is a powerful feature that allows you to dictate text directly into your document. This can be a significant time-saver for users who prefer speaking over typing or need to input large amounts of text quickly.

Using Voice Typing

1. **Activating Voice Typing:**
   - **Open Voice Typing:**
     - Click "Tools" in the menu bar.
     - Select "Voice typing..." from the dropdown menu (or press Ctrl+Shift+S).
   - **Enable Microphone Access:**
     - A microphone icon will appear on the left side of your document. Click on it to enable microphone access. If prompted, allow Google Docs to access your microphone.
2. **Dictating Text:**
   - **Start Dictating:**
     - Click the microphone icon to start voice typing. Speak clearly and at a moderate pace. The spoken words will appear as text in your document.
   - **Pause and Resume:**
     - Click the microphone icon again to pause voice typing. Click it once more to resume.
3. **Commands for Editing and Formatting:**
   - **Basic Commands:**

- Use voice commands to edit and format text without using the keyboard. For example:
    - "Select [word/phrase]"
    - "Bold"
    - "Italicize"
    - "Underline"
- **Punctuation and Formatting:**
    - You can also dictate punctuation and formatting commands:
        - "Period"
        - "Comma"
        - "New line"
        - "New paragraph"
- **Advanced Commands:**
    - Google Docs supports more advanced voice commands for editing and formatting, such as:
        - "Insert table"
        - "Insert link"
        - "Go to end of paragraph"

By using the voice typing feature, you can efficiently input text and perform basic formatting through voice commands, making it easier to create and edit documents hands-free. In the next section, we'll explore the use of add-ons and integrations to extend the functionality of Google Docs.

Add-ons and Integrations

Google Docs supports a variety of add-ons that can extend its functionality, as well as integrations with other tools and services. These features enable you to customize Google Docs to meet your specific needs and streamline your workflows.

Installing and Using Add-ons

1. **Accessing the Add-ons Menu:**
   - **Open the Add-ons Menu:**
     - Click "Extensions" in the menu bar.
     - Select "Add-ons" and then "Get add-ons."
   - **Browse and Search for Add-ons:**
     - A new window will open, displaying the Google Workspace Marketplace. You can browse popular add-ons or use the search bar to find specific ones.
2. **Installing Add-ons:**
   - **Select an Add-on:**
     - Click on an add-on to view more details, including user reviews and screenshots.
   - **Install the Add-on:**
     - Click the "Install" button and follow the prompts to grant the necessary permissions.
     - Once installed, the add-on will be accessible from the "Add-ons" menu in Google Docs.
3. **Using Add-ons:**

- Accessing Installed Add-ons:
    - Click "Extensions" in the menu bar.
    - Select "Add-ons" and choose the installed add-on you want to use.
- Interacting with Add-ons:
    - Each add-on will have its own interface and options. Follow the on-screen instructions to use the features provided by the add-on.

Popular Add-ons for Google Docs

1. **Grammarly:**
    - **Purpose:**
        - Enhances your writing by providing grammar, spelling, and style suggestions.
    - **How to Use:**
        - After installing, Grammarly will automatically check your document and highlight issues. Click on the suggestions to apply changes.
2. **DocuSign:**
    - **Purpose:**
        - Allows you to sign documents electronically and request signatures from others.
    - **How to Use:**
        - Open DocuSign from the add-ons menu, upload your document, and follow the steps to add and manage signatures.
3. **Google Translate:**
    - **Purpose:**

- Translates selected text within your document into different languages.
    - **How to Use:**
        - Highlight the text you want to translate, open Google Translate from the add-ons menu, and choose the target language.

Integrating with Other Tools

1. **Connecting with Google Sheets and Google Slides:**
    - **Embedding Content:**
        - You can embed charts from Google Sheets and slides from Google Slides directly into your Google Docs document. Click "Insert" in the menu bar, then choose "Chart" or "Slides" and follow the prompts to select the content you want to embed.
    - **Linked Content:**
        - When you link content from Google Sheets or Slides, updates made in the original document will be reflected in the linked content in Google Docs.
2. **Using Third-Party Integrations:**
    - **Zapier:**
        - **Purpose:**
            - Automates workflows by connecting Google Docs with other apps and services.
        - **How to Use:**
            - Set up Zaps (automated workflows) on the Zapier

platform to integrate Google Docs with tools like Trello, Slack, and more.
- IFTTT (If This Then That):
  - **Purpose:**
    - Creates simple automation rules between Google Docs and other services.
  - **How to Use:**
    - Create applets on the IFTTT platform to trigger actions based on changes in your Google Docs documents.

By leveraging add-ons and integrations, you can significantly enhance the functionality of Google Docs and create a more efficient and customized workflow. In the next section, we'll explore the use of Google Apps Script to automate tasks and further extend the capabilities of Google Docs.

Scripting and Automation

Google Apps Script allows you to write custom scripts to automate tasks and enhance the functionality of Google Docs. This powerful tool can help you save time, reduce errors, and streamline your workflows by automating repetitive tasks.

Using Google Apps Script

1. **Accessing Google Apps Script:**
   - **Open the Script Editor:**
     - Click "Extensions" in the menu bar.
     - Select "Apps Script." This will open the Google Apps Script editor in a new tab.
2. **Writing and Running Scripts:**
   - **Creating a New Script:**
     - In the script editor, you can start writing your script using JavaScript.
     - Google Apps Script provides a range of built-in services and methods to interact with Google Docs and other Google Workspace apps.
   - **Running Your Script:**
     - Click the "Run" button (play icon) in the script editor to execute your script.
     - The first time you run a script, you may need to authorize it to access your Google account and data.
3. **Example: Automating Document Formatting:**

Script to Format Text:
javascript
Copy code

```javascript
function formatDocument() {

  var body =
DocumentApp.getActiveDocument().getBody();

  var paragraphs = body.getParagraphs();


  for (var i = 0; i < paragraphs.length;
i++) {

    var paragraph = paragraphs[i];


paragraph.setFontFamily('Arial').setFontSiz
e(12).setForegroundColor('#000000');

    if (i === 0) {


paragraph.setHeading(DocumentApp.ParagraphH
eading.HEADING1);

    }

  }

}
```

○

- Explanation:
    - This script formats all paragraphs in the document to use the Arial font, size 12, and black color.
    - The first paragraph is set as a heading.

Setting Up Triggers

1. **Creating Triggers:**
    - **Accessing the Trigger Menu:**
        - In the script editor, click the clock icon to open the Triggers menu.
    - **Adding a Trigger:**
        - Click "Add Trigger" and configure the trigger settings:
            - **Choose which function to run:** Select the function you want to automate.
            - **Select event type:** Choose an event type (e.g., time-driven, on open, on edit).
        - Click "Save" to create the trigger.
2. **Example: Automating a Daily Task:**

Script for Daily Task:
javascript
Copy code

```javascript
function dailyTask() {

  var doc =
DocumentApp.openById('your-document-id');

  var body = doc.getBody();
```

```
body.appendParagraph('Daily update: ' +
new Date());

}
```

- ○
- ○ **Explanation:**
  - This script opens a specific Google Docs document by its ID and appends a paragraph with the current date.
- ○ **Setting Up the Trigger:**
  - In the Triggers menu, set the function `dailyTask` to run daily at a specified time.

By using Google Apps Script, you can create custom automations tailored to your specific needs, enhancing your productivity and the functionality of Google Docs. In the next section, we'll discuss collaborating and sharing features to ensure effective teamwork and document management.

Collaborating and Sharing

Google Docs offers powerful collaboration features that allow multiple users to work on a single document simultaneously. This section will guide you through the various collaboration and sharing options available, including setting permissions, adding comments, tracking changes, and more.

Introduction

Google Docs enables real-time collaboration, making it an excellent tool for team projects and collaborative writing. With features like shared access, commenting, and suggestion mode, you can work seamlessly with others, ensuring that everyone is on the same page.

Sharing Documents with Others

1. **Step-by-Step Guide to Sharing a Document:**
   - **Open the Document:**
     - Ensure your document is saved in Google Drive.
   - **Click the Share Button:**
     - In the top-right corner of the screen, click the blue "Share" button.
   - **Add People:**
     - Enter the email addresses of the people you want to share the document with.
     - You can also generate a shareable link by clicking "Get shareable link."
   - **Set Permissions:**

- Choose the permission level for each person:
  - **Viewer:** Can view but not make any changes.
  - **Commenter:** Can view and add comments but not edit the content.
  - **Editor:** Can view, comment, and make changes to the content.
  - **Send Invitations:**
    - After setting permissions, click "Send" to notify the users via email.

2. **Sharing Settings and Permissions:**
   - **Changing Permissions:**
     - To change permissions after sharing, click "Share" again, then click on the pencil icon next to a person's name to adjust their access level.
   - **Remove Access:**
     - To remove someone's access, click the "X" next to their name in the sharing settings window.
   - **Advanced Sharing Settings:**
     - Click "Advanced" in the sharing settings window to see more options, such as preventing editors from changing access and adding new people, or disabling options to download, print, and copy for commenters and viewers.

Adding Comments and Notes

1. **Adding and Managing Comments:**

- Inserting Comments:
  - Select the text or place the cursor where you want to add a comment.
  - Click the comment button in the toolbar (or press Ctrl+Alt+M).
  - Type your comment in the dialog box and click "Comment."
- Replying to and Resolving Comments:
  - Click on a comment to expand it.
  - Type your reply in the reply box and press Enter.
  - Once a comment has been addressed, click "Resolve" to mark it as resolved.

2. **Viewing and Tracking Changes:**
   - See All Comments:
     - Click the "Comments" button in the top-right corner to view all comments.
   - Managing Comments:
     - Use the "Comments" panel to navigate through comments, reply to them, and manage their status.

Real-Time Collaboration

1. **Chatting in Real-Time:**
   - In-Sheet Chat:
     - If multiple users are working on the document simultaneously, a chat icon will appear in the top-right corner. Click the icon to open a chat window and communicate in real-time.
2. **Using Suggestion Mode for Edits:**

- Activating Suggestion Mode:
  - Click the editing mode dropdown in the top-right corner (next to the "Share" button) and select "Suggesting."
- Making Suggested Edits:
  - Make edits to the document as you normally would. Your changes will appear as suggestions, highlighted in green, with the original text remaining visible.
- Accepting or Rejecting Suggestions:
  - Click on any suggestion to see the proposed changes.
  - Click the checkmark button next to the suggestion to accept it and apply the changes to the document.
  - Click the X button next to the suggestion to reject it and discard the proposed changes.

Using Notifications

1. Set Up and Manage Notifications:
   - Enabling Email Notifications:
     - Click on the "Comments" button in the top-right corner of the document.
     - Select "Notification settings."
     - Choose your preferred notification settings and click "OK."
   - Managing Notification Rules:
     - Click "Tools" in the menu bar.
     - Select "Notification rules."
     - Choose the criteria and frequency for notifications and click "Save."

By fully leveraging these collaboration and sharing features, you can enhance teamwork, maintain data accuracy, and ensure efficient project management within Google Docs. In the next section, we'll discuss advanced features to help you make the most of Google Docs.

Advanced Features

Google Docs offers a variety of advanced features that can help you create more sophisticated documents, improve your workflow, and increase productivity. This section will cover the use of advanced formatting and styling, creating and using templates, and the benefits of utilizing Google Apps Script for automation.

Using Add-ons and Integrations

1. **Installing and Using Add-ons:**
   - **Accessing the Add-ons Menu:**
     - Click "Extensions" in the menu bar.
     - Select "Add-ons" and then "Get add-ons."
   - **Browse and Search for Add-ons:**
     - Use the Google Workspace Marketplace to browse or search for specific add-ons.
   - **Installing Add-ons:**
     - Click on an add-on to view more details.
     - Click "Install" and follow the prompts to grant permissions.
     - Access installed add-ons from the "Extensions" menu.
2. **Popular Add-ons for Google Docs:**
   - **Grammarly:**
     - Enhances writing by providing grammar, spelling, and style suggestions.
     - Automatically checks your document and highlights issues.

- DocuSign:
  - Allows electronic signatures and signature requests.
  - Upload your document and follow the steps to manage signatures.
- Google Translate:
  - Translates selected text within your document into different languages.
  - Highlight the text, open Google Translate from the add-ons menu, and choose the target language.

Advanced Formatting and Styling

1. **Creating and Using Templates:**
   - **Creating a Template:**
     - Design your document with the desired formatting and elements.
     - Save the document as a template by clicking "File," then "Make a copy."
   - **Using a Template:**
     - Open the template document and make a copy for each new project or document.
     - Customize the copy as needed without altering the original template.
2. **Customizing Styles and Themes:**
   - **Custom Styles:**
     - Format text with desired attributes (font, size, color, etc.).
     - Save custom styles by updating the styles menu (e.g., "Normal text," "Heading 1").
   - **Themes:**

- Apply consistent styling across documents by creating a theme with specific fonts, colors, and formatting rules.
- Save and reuse themes for brand consistency and professional appearance.

Using Google Apps Script

1. **Writing and Running Scripts:**
   - **Accessing the Script Editor:**
     - Click "Extensions" in the menu bar.
     - Select "Apps Script" to open the script editor in a new tab.
   - **Creating a New Script:**
     - Write your script using JavaScript.
     - Use built-in services and methods to interact with Google Docs and other Google Workspace apps.
   - **Running Your Script:**
     - Click the "Run" button (play icon) in the script editor to execute your script.
     - Authorize the script to access your Google account and data if prompted.
2. **Example: Automating Document Processes:**

Automate Formatting:
javascript
Copy code

```javascript
function automateFormatting() {
```

```
    var body =
DocumentApp.getActiveDocument().getBody();


body.setFontFamily('Arial').setFontSize(12)
;

    var paragraphs = body.getParagraphs();

    for (var i = 0; i < paragraphs.length;
i++) {

        var paragraph = paragraphs[i];

        if (i === 0) {


paragraph.setHeading(DocumentApp.ParagraphH
eading.HEADING1);

        }

    }

}
```

- ○
  - ○ **Setting Up Triggers:**
    - ■ Access the Trigger menu by clicking the clock icon in the script editor.
    - ■ Set the function to run automatically based on events (e.g., time-driven, on open, on edit).

By leveraging these advanced features, you can enhance the functionality and efficiency of Google Docs, making it a more powerful tool for your projects and workflows. In the next section, we'll provide a practical example of creating a project documentation template to illustrate how these features can be applied in a real-world scenario.

Practical Example: Creating a Project Documentation Template

Creating a project documentation template in Google Docs can help streamline your project management process by providing a consistent format for documenting project details, progress, and outcomes. This section will guide you through the steps to set up and customize your template.

Step 1: Document Setup

1. **Preparing Your Document:**
   - **Create a New Document:**
     - Open Google Docs and create a new document by clicking "Blank" in the Template Gallery.
   - **Title and Introduction:**
     - Add a title for your project documentation template (e.g., "Project Documentation Template").
     - Write a brief introduction that outlines the purpose and scope of the document.
2. **Setting Up Styles and Formatting:**
   - **Define Heading Styles:**
     - Format the main headings (e.g., Project Overview, Project Plan, Progress Report) using "Heading 1."
     - Use "Heading 2" for subheadings (e.g., Objectives, Timeline, Tasks).

- Create Custom Styles:
    - Highlight formatted text and update the style in the styles dropdown to ensure consistency throughout the document.

Step 2: Inserting Tables and Images

1. **Adding Tables for Data Organization:**
    - **Insert a Table:**
        - Click "Insert" in the menu bar and select "Table."
        - Choose the number of rows and columns needed for your data (e.g., a 5x5 table for tasks and deadlines).
    - **Formatting Tables:**
        - Adjust the table's appearance by changing border colors, cell background colors, and text alignment.
2. **Inserting and Formatting Images:**
    - **Add Images:**
        - Click "Insert" in the menu bar and select "Image," then choose an image from your computer or the web.
    - **Format Images:**
        - Resize and position the image as needed.
        - Add captions or labels to provide context for the image.

Step 3: Adding Links and Bookmarks

1. **Creating Hyperlinks for Reference:**

- o **Insert a Link:**
  - ■ Highlight the text you want to turn into a hyperlink.
  - ■ Click the link button in the toolbar (or press Ctrl+K).
  - ■ Enter the URL and click "Apply."
2. **Using Bookmarks for Navigation:**
   - o **Insert a Bookmark:**
     - ■ Place your cursor where you want to add the bookmark.
     - ■ Click "Insert" in the menu bar and select "Bookmark."
   - o **Link to Bookmarks:**
     - ■ Highlight the text you want to link.
     - ■ Click the link button, select "Bookmarks," and choose the bookmark to link to.

Step 4: Using Comments and Suggestions

1. **Collaborating with Team Members:**
   - o **Add Comments:**
     - ■ Highlight text and click the comment button in the toolbar (or press Ctrl+Alt+M).
     - ■ Type your comment and click "Comment."
   - o **Reply to Comments:**
     - ■ Click on an existing comment and type your reply.
2. **Managing Feedback and Edits:**
   - o **Use Suggestion Mode:**
     - ■ Click the editing mode dropdown in the top-right corner and select "Suggesting."

- Make edits that appear as suggestions, which can be accepted or rejected by collaborators.

Example Layout

1. **Top Section: Project Overview:**
   - Title: "Project Documentation Template"
   - Introduction: Brief outline of the document's purpose and scope.
   - Project Overview: Description, objectives, and key stakeholders.
2. **Middle Section: Detailed Descriptions:**
   - Project Plan: Timeline, milestones, and tasks.
   - Progress Report: Status updates, completed tasks, and next steps.
3. **Bottom Section: Additional Resources:**
   - Attachments: Links to related documents and resources.
   - Contact Information: Details for project leads and key contacts.

Screenshot Examples (Illustrative)

1. **Document Setup:**
   - Screenshot of the initial setup with title and headings.
2. **Tables and Images:**
   - Screenshot showing a table with formatted cells and an inserted image.
3. **Links and Bookmarks:**
   - Screenshot demonstrating hyperlinks and bookmarks in the document.
4. **Comments and Suggestions:**

- Screenshot displaying comments and suggested edits.

Step 5: Sharing and Collaboration

1. **Sharing the Document with Team Members:**
   - Click the "Share" button and enter email addresses.
   - Set permissions (Viewer, Commenter, Editor) and send invitations.
2. **Enabling Real-Time Collaboration:**
   - Collaborators can work simultaneously, leave comments, and suggest edits.
   - Use the "Comments" and "Suggestion Mode" features to manage feedback and changes.

Step 6: Automating with Google Apps Script

1. **Writing a Script for Automatic Updates:**

Example Script: Add a timestamp each time the document is edited.
javascript
Copy code

```javascript
function addTimestamp() {

  var doc =
DocumentApp.getActiveDocument();

  var body = doc.getBody();

  body.appendParagraph('Document updated
on: ' + new Date());
```

}

- ○
2. **Setting Up Triggers for the Script:**
    - ○ Access the Trigger menu in the script editor.
    - ○ Set the function to run based on specific events (e.g., time-driven, on open).

By following these steps, you can create a comprehensive and professional project documentation template in Google Docs. This template will help ensure consistency and efficiency in your project management process.

Conclusion

Google Docs is a versatile and powerful tool for document creation and collaboration. Throughout this guide, we've explored the essential features and advanced functionalities that make Google Docs a valuable resource for both personal and professional use.

Recap of Key Features and Tools:

1. **Basic and Advanced Text Formatting:**
   - Customize fonts, sizes, colors, and paragraph alignment.
   - Utilize headers, footers, and page numbers for a polished look.
2. **Inserting Elements:**
   - Enhance documents with images, tables, and links.
   - Use bookmarks for easy navigation within long documents.
3. **Comments and Suggestions:**
   - Collaborate effectively with real-time comments and suggestion mode.
   - Resolve feedback and manage edits efficiently.
4. **Revision History:**
   - Track changes and restore previous versions of your document.
5. **Using Notifications:**
   - Stay informed about document changes and comments through email notifications.
6. **Voice Typing:**
   - Dictate text and use voice commands for hands-free document creation.

7. **Add-ons and Integrations:**
   - Extend functionality with popular add-ons like Grammarly and DocuSign.
   - Integrate with other Google Workspace apps and third-party tools.
8. **Scripting and Automation:**
   - Automate tasks with Google Apps Script.
   - Set up triggers for repetitive processes to save time.
9. **Collaborating and Sharing:**
   - Share documents with customized permissions.
   - Enable real-time collaboration and communication within the document.
10. **Advanced Features:**
    - Create and use templates for consistency.
    - Customize styles and themes for professional-looking documents.
11. **Practical Applications:**
    - Apply your skills to practical tasks such as report writing, project documentation, marketing materials, meeting minutes, and educational tools.

Encouragement to Explore and Utilize Google Docs Fully:

Google Docs offers a wealth of features that can enhance your productivity and streamline your workflows. By mastering both the basic and advanced capabilities, you can create professional documents with ease, collaborate effectively with others, and automate repetitive tasks to save time.

Whether you're a student, professional, or casual user, Google Docs provides the flexibility and tools you need to succeed. Take the time to explore and experiment with its features, and you'll discover new ways to improve your document creation and collaboration processes.

Final Thoughts:

We hope this guide has provided you with a comprehensive understanding of Google Docs and its capabilities. By leveraging the information and examples provided, you can make the most of this powerful tool and achieve your document-related goals efficiently and effectively.

Thank you for using this guide, and happy writing with Google Docs!

www.ingramcontent.com/pod-product-compliance
Lightning Source LLC
LaVergne TN
LVHW051622050326
832903LV00033B/4618